Dolph

A 3D Guide to Oceanic Dolphins and Porpoises

Written and Illustrated by

Ian Ringrose

Layout and Typesetting by Sarah Williams

Individually Printed and Hand Finished in Oxford, England

A Wild3D Publication

www.wild3d.com

Published by Wild3D.

First Edition Published 2007

ISBN: 978-0-9549881-1-1

Contents

Dolphin Illustrations

Preface

I have spent much of my life working in the marine field; initially as a seaman and more recently with 3D graphic systems for mariner training. This experience, coupled with a long-standing interest in marine life, has resulted in 'Dolphins In 3D', a new approach to stimulating awareness in these beautiful and diverse creatures and the conservation problems which may influence their future.

The book is designed to be used with a PC on your desktop. It is small, robust and contains a CD with easy-to-follow instructions for loading 3D illustrations of the dolphins. These take the form of interactive, animated 3D graphic windows that provide a dynamic 3D perspective of each type of dolphin on your computer screen. Supporting text includes basic facts about each species in the oceanic dolphin (Delphinidae) and porpoise (Phocoenidae) families. Many excellent in-depth references exist which detail dolphin anatomy, behaviour etc and a further reading section is added to the appendices with one or two of my personal favourites.

Despite the small format, Sarah and I decided to leave plenty of white space for adding your own ideas, notes, scribbles, sketches (and coffee stains). The CD also has space for recording files and folders which may be acquired online or from colleagues who share your interest in dolphins.

Finally, the book details ways of including the 3D illustrations in projects and websites with the specific intention of increasing awareness in dolphins and the important conservation issues that currently affect their future.

Ian Ringrose PhD
Oxford, England
Spring 2007

Dolphin Anatomy

The following anatomical features help identify the different species of dolphin.

Chapter 1

Setting Up Your PC

Before starting to read this book it is necessary to copy data from the 'Dolphins In 3D' CD to your PC so that it can display 3D dolphin illustrations.

Copying the CD

To copy dolphin 3D data to your PC, remove the CD from the back of the book and place it in the CD/DVD drive on your computer. Open the CD/DVD drive window and drag the 'Dolphins In 3D' folder to your PC desktop. Open this folder and open file 'Dolphin Index' to view the dolphin index page.

Navigating 3D Illustrations

Each thumbnail image on the index file corresponds to an equivalent figure in the book. As a trial, move the cursor over the first thumbnail. Descriptive text appears which specifies both the figure number and name of dolphin. Click once to display the Common Bottlenose dolphin 3D window and again to start moving the image.

To rotate the view, click and hold down the mouse left button within the window and move it left, right, up and down. To zoom in and out, click and hold the mouse right button and move it up and down. To move the view from side to side or up and down, click and hold down both buttons.

Note: The software used to display 3D illustrations requires Java to be installed on your PC. If a figure is selected and the dolphin doesn't appear, use the download link provided in the window to connect and download the latest version of Java at www.java.com.

3D Animations

The final group of thumbnail images, in the Dolphin Index show animated 3D movies, which comprise various species of dolphin in different marine settings. They are non-interactive and are displayed using Start/Stop/Rewind controls in Microsoft Media Player. The scenes are arranged to match different species of dolphin with geographical locations and habitats.

Drag-and-Drop Dolphins In 3D folder to your desktop

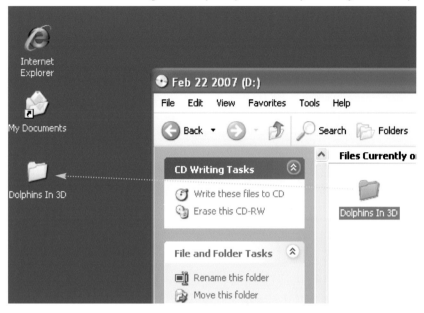

Select and display a dolphin 3D window using the Dolphin Index

DOLPHIN INDEX PAGE

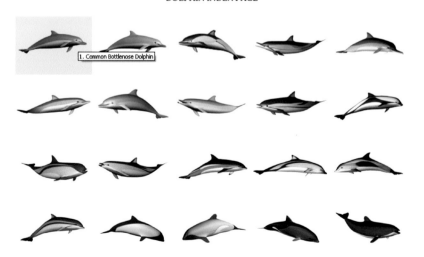

Control the 3D dolphin using your mouse buttons

Common Bottlenose Dolphin

Click-and-Hold

Left Button   - To Rotate
Right Button - To Zoom
Both Buttons - To Translate

Control 3D animations using Windows Media Player

Chapter 2

Dolphin Species

Common Bottlenose Dolphin

Tursiops truncatus

Other Names Bottle-nosed dolphin, Atlantic Bottlenose dolphin.

Description Large, robust dolphin with light underside and shaded grey body. It has a round, well-formed melon, darker shading on the cape and a stocky snout with prominent triangular dorsal fin. Faint striping is often present from the front of the melon to the eye and also from the eye to the pectoral fins.

Habitat Widely distributed throughout tropical and temperate oceans. It is particularly prominent along coasts and inshore waters and can also be found in enclosed seas such as the Mediterranean. Some areas of its geographical range are shared with the Indo-Pacific Bottlenose Dolphin.

Behaviour An intelligent, social species which lives in complex societies ranging from around 10 to 15 individuals inshore to hundreds in the open ocean. Curious of humans, they often show great interest in boats, swimmers and divers and will readily bow-ride passing vessels. Social co-operation makes them a very successful species, particularly in hunting where techniques used are adapted to suit pre-vailing circumstances and local habitat. Only the Orca has a more varied diet. They are comfortable in the company of other cetaceans and are often seen swimming with pilot whales. Their large size often leads to 'bullying' smaller species and in some cases Bottlenose dolphins have been known to kill young dolphins and porpoises.

Reproduction Calves every 3-6 years, gestation twelve months.

Diet Wide variety of fish, squid, shrimp, krill and other crus-taceans.

Threats Hunting, loss of habitat, chemical pollution, entanglement in fish nets, captivity industry and loss of habitat.

Max length 3.8 m.

Max weight 600 kg.

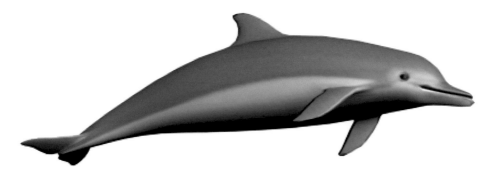

1. Common Bottlenose Dolphin

Indo-Pacific Bottlenose Dolphin

Tursiops aduncus

Other Names Bottle-nosed dolphin, Pacific Bottlenose dolphin.

Description Long, slender body with light underside and shaded light grey sides. It has a dark cape and may have spots on the underside and/or flanks. Faint striping is often present from the front of the melon to the eye and it also has a distinct melon crease.

Habitat Found in shallow tropical or temperate waters around the Indian and Western Pacific Ocean rims. Its distribution overlaps significantly with the Common Bottlenose.

Behaviour Smaller and less robust than its namesake the Common Dolphin, Indo-Pacific Bottlenose dolphins live almost exclusively in shallow, coastal waters where they clan together into small groups of up to fifteen individuals. They have only recently been recognised as a separate species and may have genetic roots in the Spotted or Striped dolphin families. Intelligent and versatile, the Indo-Pacific Bottlenose will adapt to local environments and vary its hunting techniques accordingly. Always a 'social' hunter, they seem equally at home burrowing in the seabed for small fish or invertibrates as they do when they are chasing and herding large shoals. It can often be seen swimming with other species including Common Bottlenose and Pacific White-sided Dolphins.

Reproduction Calves every 3-6 years, gestation twelve months.

Diet Wide variety of fish, squid, shrimp, krill and other crustaceans.

Threats As a coastal species it is primarily at risk from loss of habitat. It is also hunted for food in the Phillipines.

Max length 2.6 m.

Max weight 230 kg.

2. Indo-Pacific Bottlenose Dolphin

Short-beaked Common Dolphin

Delphinus delphis

Other Names Criss-cross dolphin, Saddleback dolphin, White-bellied porpoise.

Description Streamlined body with criss-cross grey and yellow pattern on flank. It has a black or black/brown cape with white underside and a black stripe from beak to pectoral fins. Striping also occurs around the chin.

Habitat Found in tropical, subtropical and warm temperate waters of the Atlantic and Pacific Ocean. It is the most numerous dolphin species in these waters and is also found in the Mediterranean and Black Seas. Generally prefers deep water.

Behaviour In 1994, after much confusion, the Common dolphin was finally divided into two separate species; Short and Long-beaked. Difficult to distinguish at sea, the Short-beaked Common dolphin has a higher contrast colour pattern and a more robust shape. They often travel in groups which vary from 10 to 500 individuals. This can increase to 2000 in some areas of the eastern Pacific. Exuberant, noisy and acrobatic, they often bow-ride passing vessels and can be heard underwater over large distances.

Reproduction Calves every 2-3 years, gestation 10-11 months.

Diet Variety of schooling fish and marine invertebrates such as herring, anchovies, sardines and squid.

Threats They are seen as a threat to fishing in the Black Sea and are killed in large numbers by Russian and Turkish fishermen. They are prone to drowning in drift nets and are also affected by deep-water offshore pollution.

Max length 2.7 m.

Max weight 150 kg.

Long-beaked Common Dolphin

Delphinus capensis

Other Names Criss-cross dolphin, Saddleback dolphin, White-bellied porpoise.

Description Streamlined body with criss-cross grey and yellow pattern on flank. Black cape with white underside and a black stripe from beak to flippers. They are more streamlined than the Short-beaked Common dolphin, have a comparatively long beak and have a more muted colour pattern.

Habitat Found in tropical, subtropical and warm temperate waters of the Atlantic, Pacific and Indian Oceans. It is not so numerous as the Short-beaked variety and unlike its namesake it is more commonly found in warm, shallow, coastal waters.

Behaviour In 1994, after much confusion, the Common dolphin was finally divided into two separate species; Short and Long-beaked. Difficult to distinguish at sea, the Long-beaked Common dolphin has a more muted colour pattern and slender shape. Despite their differences in habitat, Long and Short-beaked Common dolphins are often seen swimming together in groups which can include hundreds of individuals.

Reproduction Calves every 2-3 years, gestation 10-11 months.

Diet Variety of schooling fish such as herring, anchovies and sardines.

Threats They are certainly hunted off Peru and probably elsewhere.

Max length 2.5 m.

Max weight 150 kg.

4. Long-beaked Common Dolphin

Spinner Dolphin

Stenella longirostris

Other Names Long-snouted dolphin, Long-beaked dolphin.

Description Varies greatly in appearance from one region to another. Shape, size, colouring and even behaviour can be different. Generally, it has a three-tier pattern with a dark grey cape, mid-grey flanks and white underside. The dorsal fin is erect and slightly falcate and they often have a dark stripe from the eye to the pectoral fins. Spinners are slender, very streamlined and have an exceptionally long beak.

Habitat Predominantly found in tropical and sub-tropical waters worldwide but may also be found in warmer temperate seas. It is a deep ocean species but may occasionally be seen close to the coast. Despite considerable depletion due to fishing, it is still one of the more common species.

Behaviour The most acrobatic of all dolphins, it is so-named because of its incredible high spinning leaps. It may breach and spin several times before finally plunging back into the water. This behaviour is fre-quently seen far out to sea on the front of long ocean swells.

Reproduction Calves every three years, gestation 10-11 months.

Diet Fish and squid.

Threats Spinner dolphin numbers have fallen dramatically due to the tuna fishery. They are either drowned in the gill nets or hauled aboard, killed and discarded by the fishermen. Despite efforts to prevent this, thousands are still killed and eastern stocks in Asia and Australia are probably only half of what they were originally.

Max length 2.4 m.

Max weight 90 kg.

Clymene Dolphin

Stenella clymene

Other Names Short-snouted spinner dolphin, Senegal dolphin.

Description The Clymene dolphin was originally thought to be a sub-species of the Spinner. However, in 1981 it was officially classified as a separate species. Slightly smaller than the Spinner, it shares its three-tier pattern of dark grey cape, mid-grey flanks and white underside. It has a marked stripe which extends from the eye to dark slender flippers.

Habitat Found in warmer tropical and sub-tropical waters of the Atlantic Ocean. It is a deep water dolphin that is rarely seen close to shore and for this reason little is actually known about the species. Its range does overlap with the Spinner dolphin and they are often seen swimming together.

Behaviour A social species that are usually observed in schools of 50 or more individuals. Larger groups which contain hundreds of dolphins are not unusual. Strandings indicate that sexes may swim together i.e. they are almost always one sex or the other. Clymene dolphins 'spin' but not so often or acrobatically as the Spinner. They are, however, keen bow-riders and have been observed deliberately changing course to accompany a boat or ship.

Reproduction No Information.

Diet Fish and squid.

Threats Little is known about the numbers of Clymene dolphins. Some hunting takes place in the Caribbean and they have been found in gill nets off the West African coast.

Max length 2 m.

Max weight 80 kg.

6. Clymene Dolphin

Atlantic Spotted Dolphin

Stenella frontalis

Other Names Spotted dolphin.

Description There are many variations from lightly spotted on the underside to almost completely covered with spots. In general, they have a robust, streamlined shape with dark spots on the underside and lighter spots on the cape. Young dolphins don't have spots; they develop with age. Like the Spinner, they usually (not always) have a three-tier colour pattern, with a dark grey cape, mid-grey flank and white underside. Most also have a diagonal blaze that sweeps through the cape towards the dorsal fin.

Habitat Found in temperate, sub-tropical and tropical waters of the Atlantic Ocean. The extent of their range is about 50° North and 25° South. It is thought to be a coastal species but deep water sightings are not unusual.

Behaviour A social species that are usually observed in smaller schools of ten or more individuals. It has been the subject of numerous studies in the Bahamas region of the Caribbean Sea, though little is know about their behaviour in deep water.

Reproduction Calves every three years, gestation 10-11 months.

Diet Fish, squid and other small invertebrates.

Threats It is hunted for bait in South America and often killed in nets in the Caribbean and West Africa.

Max length 2.3 m.

Max weight 140 kg.

7. Atlantic Spotted Dolphin

Pantropical Spotted Dolphin

Stenella attenuata

Other Names Spotted dolphin.

Description There is a lot of variation in the appearance of this species. It generally has an elongated, slender shape with a dark cape and white underside. Adult dolphins can be heavily spotted whereas young have none. Spots can fuse and fade as the dolphin gets older. The beak is long and narrow and there is usually a dark stripe from beak to pectoral fin. It has a tall, falcate dorsal fin.

Habitat Found worldwide in tropical and some sub-tropical waters of the Atlantic, Pacific and Indian Oceans. They are abundant in equitorial seas but have been observed between latitudes 40° North and 40° South of the equator. Can be found in shallow coastal waters or in the deep ocean. Coastal dolphins are generally larger, more robust and have more spots.

Behaviour Though not as acrobatic as the Spinner, this species frequently breaches with high, vertical leaps. They are often seen swimming with shoals of Tuna and many thousands are killed in Tuna nets every year. Efforts to stop the slaughter, such as new release techniques, have only been partially successful. The reasons for this behaviour is still not clear, but the Tuna may improve their chances of finding fish shoals.

Reproduction Calves every 2-4 years, gestation 11-12 months.

Diet Fish, squid and other small crustaceans.

Threats Despite being hunted in many parts of the world and also caught in Tuna nets, the Pantropical Spotted dolphin is still fairly abundant.

Max length 2.6 m.

Max weight 120 kg.

8. Pantropical Spotted Dolphin

Striped Dolphin

Stenella coeruleoalba

Other Names Streaker.

Description Very distinctive dolphin with dark blue cape, shaded blue/white flanks with long prominent dark blue stripe. The underside is white and sometimes has a pinkish hue. It has a stripe from eye to pectoral fin. A pale blue shoulder blaze sweeps up towards a prominent, falcate, dorsal fin.

Habitat Found worldwide, but most common in tropical, subtropical and warmer temperate waters. Observed as far north as Greenland and Iceland, the Striped dolphin is the most numerous cetacean in the Mediterranean Sea, where they are often caught in deep water drift-nets. Sub-species exist in shallow coastal waters and also in the deep ocean.

Behaviour A conspicuous, acrobatic dolphin which spends much of its time performing a variety of breaches, belly-flops, back somersaults and tail spins. Their distinctive stripes and great speed has prompted the name 'streakers'. In some (but not all) parts of the world they bow-ride passing boats and ships. Striped dolphins are very social and in the deep ocean they group together into very large schools which can amount to hundreds of individuals.

Reproduction Calves every four years, gestation 12-13 months.

Diet Fish and squid.

Threats They are hunted in Asia (particularly Japan) but are mainly threatened by entanglement in fishing nets.

Max length 2.7 m.

Max weight 160 kg.

9. Striped Dolphin

Hourglass Dolphin
Lagenorhynchus cruciger

Other Names Sea Skunk.

Description A small, robust dolphin with very distinctive black-and-white 'hourglass' shaped markings on its flanks. It has a short black beak, black flukes, black pectoral fins and large black falcate dorsal fin.

Habitat A cold water dolphin found in remote Antarctic and Sub-Antarctic seas between 45° and 60° South. Little is known about this species which is often observed bow-riding cruise ships travelling to and from Antarctica. Its striking markings and prominent dorsal fin make it easy to identify. Though oceanic by nature, sightings of this dolphin have been recorded close to shore in isolated islands such as the South Shetlands.

Behaviour Hourglass dolphins are thought to live in small groups of up to ten individuals but have been recorded in schools of around 100. It has been seen swimming with fin whales, pilot whales and right-whale dolphins and has also been recorded feeding with large gatherings of seabirds.

Reproduction Calves every four years, gestation 12-13 months.

Diet Fish and squid.

Threats None recorded.

Max length 1.9 m.

Max weight 95 kg.

24

Peale's Dolphin

Lagenorhynchus australis

Other Names Blackchin Dolphin.

Description Robust body with black dorsal fin, back and upper flanks with a grey steak running to the tail. It has grey lower flanks and a white belly. Peale's dolphin closely resembles the Dusky dolphin but has a darker head and white spots under its pectoral fins.

Habitat Found in straits, fjords, inlets and along the continental shelf of southern South America. Its range is approximately 38° South in the Atlantic to 44° South in the Pacific. Associated with swift flowing coastal water, they are commonly seen by Antarctic cruise ships around the Tierra Del Fuego as they approach Cape Horn.

Behaviour Though capable of breaching, bow-riding and other dolphin acrobatics, Peale's dolphin is usually seen travelling slowly in small groups of up to five dolphins parallel to the shore or near kelp beds. They often accompany Commerson's dolphin which overlap in range and can group together in large schools of over 100 individuals.

Reproduction Unknown.

Diet Fish and squid, octopus and crustaceans.

Threats In the past it was heavily exploited to provide bait for catching crabs. Scale of hunting has decreased recently but unknown numbers are still harpooned.

Max length 2.2 m.

Max weight 115 kg.

Dusky Dolphin

Lagenorhynchus obscurus

Other Names None.

Description Distinctly marked, small, robust dolphin with black/grey dorsal fin, black upper flanks and two grey blazes pointing toward the head. It has light grey lower flanks, a white belly. a short black beak and white face. Their markings are very similar to the Pacific White-sided Dolphin but there is no overlap in range.

Habitat Found globally in temperate coastal and shelf waters of the southern hemisphere. Although widely scattered, they are most common in South America, New Zealand and south-west Africa. Tends to be more abundant in northern waters in the winter months and southern waters during the summer. Widespread distribution makes Dusky dolphin population estimates very difficult.

Behaviour A very social dolphin which can often be seen in the company of other species. 'Duskies' are inquisitive and frequently play with people in the water. They will readily approach boats and, in addition to bow-riding, perform a range of acrobatics, sometimes repeating their displays many times over. Groups vary from a couple of individuals to tens or hundreds. They tend to hunt in smaller groups but gather together to relax and play.

Reproduction Unknown.

Diet Fish and squid.

Threats The 'Duskies' friendly nature is not reciprocated by man and many are harpooned for food in Peru. Unknown numbers are also known to drown in fishing nets throughout their range.

Max length 2.1 m.

Max weight 90 kg.

12. Dusky Dolphin

Atlantic White-Sided Dolphin

Lagenorhynchus acutus

Other Names Lag, White-sided jumper. The term 'Lag' is used primarily by marine scientists and is a shortened reference to its Latin name *Lagenorhynchus*.

Description Boldly marked, sturdy dolphin with black upperside, a thick tail stock, a wide longitudinal grey stripe along the flanks and white belly. It has a very distinct white streak below the dorsal fin and yellow/tan streak along the side of the tail stock. The dark uppersides and yellow streak can lead to confusion with the Common dolphin, but the position of the streak on the stock and the more demarcated colouring make the Atlantic White-sided dolphin very distinctive at close distance.

Habitat Found in deep, cold Arctic and Sub-Arctic waters of the North Atlantic Ocean. Its range stretches from Northern Europe to Greenland and the shelf waters off Newfoundland, Nova Scotia and Cape Cod. Most commonly observed over the continental shelf and slope.

Behaviour A very social and gregarious species, it lives in schools of between 5 and 50 individuals. Combined groups can amount to 500 or more. It can often be seen swimming alongside boats and ships and also bow-rides faster vessels. It is frequently observed swimming with other cetaceans including fin and humpback whales.

Reproduction Calves every two years, gestation eleven months.

Diet Fish and squid.

Threats Small numbers are frequently killed around the Greenland coast and in the Faeroe Islands.

Max length 2.7 m.

Max weight 230 kg.

13. Atlantic White-sided Dolphin

Pacific White-Sided Dolphin

Lagenorhynchus obliquidens

Other Names Lag, Pacific Striped dolphin. The term 'Lag' is used primarily by marine scientists and is a shortened reference to its Latin name *Lagenorhynchus*.

Description Robust dolphin with black upperside, grey patches along the flanks and white belly. A bold black line demarcates the flanks and underside. The dorsal fin is large, falcate and is predominently grey with a black leading edge. It has a black beak, white face and dark area around the eyes.

Habitat Pacific White-sided dolphins are found in cold temperate waters across the North Pacific. A coastal species, it is frequently seen offshore in both shallow and deep water.

Behaviour Very social and gregarious, it is most often observed in large schools which may amount to hundreds or even thousands of individuals, as well as with other species of dolphin such as Risso's or Northern Rightwhale. They frequently bow-ride and are very acrobatic, breaching and per-

forming somersaults before plunging back into the water. Though remarkably similar to Dusky dolphins in appearance, they share no genetic ties and there is no overlap in the ranges of the two species.

Reproduction Possibly calves every 2-3 years, gestation twelve months.

Diet Fish and squid.

Threats Very large numbers have been killed by drift net fishermen in the North Pacific and despite recent legislation many are still drowned in nets.

Max length 2.5 m.

Max weight 180 kg.

White-beaked Dolphin

Lagenorhynchus albirostris

Other Names Squidhound.

Description Largest of the 'Lag' dolphins, it has a robust, strong body and diffuse grey, black and white markings. Its beak is often white but may also be light or dark grey. It has a white underside which may be mottled.

Habitat Found in the cool temperate and Sub-Arctic waters of the North Atlantic Ocean. Most northerly of all dolphins, its range extends from Northern Europe to Greenland and the North Eastern shores of the USA and Canada. Distribution is similar to the Atlantic White-sided dolphin but it is found further north along both coasts of Greenland and further into the Barents Sea. The White-beaked dolphin seems to prefer deeper continental shelf waters but is also frequently observed in shallow coastal waters.

Behaviour A large, acrobatic dolphin that is often observed swimming at speed. It is a social feeder and is often seen in the company of other dolphins (particularly Atlantic White-sided) and whales such as the Fin or Humpback.

Reproduction Unknown.

Diet Fish, squid, octopus and other crustaceans.

Threats Drift-net fishing.

Max length 3.1 m.

Max weight 350 kg.

Fraser's Dolphin
Lagenodelphis hosei

Other Names White-bellied dolphin, Sarawak dolphin.

Description Fraser's dolphin is usually easy to recognise, with its dark stripes and bandit-like face. It has a dark grey-blue cape, grey-blue or greenish body and white or pinkish underside. Not all have stripes but they travel in large groups and there will always be individuals that have them. A stocky, robust dolphin, they have a small triangular dorsal fin and very small pectoral fins.

Habitat Found throughout the world in deep tropical and sub-tropical waters. Rarely seen inshore except around oceanic islands and seamounts.

Behaviour Named after scientist Francis Fraser who first described the species in 1956. Relatively little is known about this dolphin due to its preference for deep water, but it is now frequently observed on dolphin watching tours in the Caribbean. They are invariably seen in large schools of 100-500 individuals, some sightings recording as many as 1000. They are also seen in the company of other, larger, dolphins. These commonly include Melon-headed whales, Short-finned Pilot whales and False Killer whales.

Reproduction Estimates suggest calves every two years, gestation 12-13 months.

Diet Fish, squid and crustaceans.

Threats Entanglement in fishing nets, some hunting in the Indo-Pacific area.

Max length 2.7 m.

Max weight 210 kg.

Commerson's Dolphin

Cephalorhynchus commersonii

Other Names Skunk dolphin, Black-and-White dolphin, Piebald dolphin.

Description Small, stocky body and very distinctive black and white pattern which varies from individual to individual. The dorsal fin is small and rounded, giving Commerson's dolphin a low profile in the water. It has a small black beak, black pectoral fins, black flukes and a black patch on its underside.

Habitat Commerson's dolphin lives in cold, shallow sub-Antarctic waters around the southern tip of South America between 41° South and 53° South. This includes the Falkland Islands, South Shetland Islands and Tierra Del Fuego. An isolated population has also been found 8,000 km away in the Indian Ocean at Kerguelen Island.

Behaviour Commerson's dolphin is porpoise-like in size and appearance but behaves very much like a dolphin. Fast swimming and acrobatic, it is often observed breaching in the coastal surf and will readily bow-ride passing ships. It also has the habit of swimming upside down, spinning round-and-round as it goes.

Reproduction Unknown.

Diet Fish and crustaceans.

Threats Entanglement in gill nets. Hunted for crab bait in Chile, though it is now illegal.

Max length 1.7 m.

Max weight 90 kg.

Hector's Dolphin

Cephalorhynchus hectori

Other Names New Zealand dolphin.

Description Very small, stocky, distinctively marked dolphin with complex black, grey and white colouring. It has broad, rounded, black dorsal and pectoral fins and a small black-tipped beak. It is the world's smallest dolphin.

Habitat Lives in small groups only around the coasts of New Zealand. Restricted to shallow water, it rarely ranges far off-shore and is frequently observed in harbours or patrolling the surfline.

Behaviour Playful and inquisitive, Hector's dolphin often bow-rides slower moving boats but rarely breach. Its small, low-profile shape makes it difficult to spot in the water, but the rounded dorsal fin makes them easy to identify. Despite government intervention, the population of Hector's dolphin has been decimated by commercial gill net fishing and it is now amongst the most endangered dolphin species.

Reproduction Estimates suggest it calves every 2-4 years, gestation 10-11 months.

Diet Fish, squid and crustaceans.

Threats Entanglement in gill nets. Collision with high speed pleasure craft.

Max length 1.6 m.

Max weight 60 kg.

18. Hector's Dolphin

Heaviside's Dolphin

Cephalorhynchus heavisidii

Other Names South African dolphin.

Description Small, stocky, distinctively marked dolphin, predominently grey towards the head and black around the tail stock and flukes. It has a brilliant white belly with finger-shaped lobes on each flank, a distinctive black triangular dorsal fin midway along its back and a black patch around the eyes.

Habitat Restricted to shallow waters along the Namibian/South African coastline from about 17° South to 34° South. Heaviside's dolphin lives exclusively in shallow water, probably not exceeding 100 m depth. It seems to prefer colder waters and is often associated with the northward flowing Benguela Current.

Behaviour Despite its small size and porpoise-like appearance, Heaviside's is one of the most acrobatic of all dolphin species. Completely at home in turbulent offshore waters or along the surfline, it will readily breach and also approach and bow-ride or wake-ride any pas-

sing vessel or boats. Although not a lot is known about this species, its playful antics are now the focus of dolphin watching tours in both Namibia and South Africa.

Reproduction Possibly calves every 2-4 years, gestation 10-11 months.

Diet Fish and possibly squid.

Threats Some local fishing.

Max length 1.7 m.

Max weight 75 kg.

19. Heaviside's Dolphin

Chilean Dolphin

Cephalorhynchus eutropia

Other Names Black dolphin.

Description Very small, stocky, distinctively marked dolphin, with a shaded black body and contrasting white underside. The grey head is conically shaped and it has a large, rounded dorsal fin. Pectoral fins and flukes are also black and it has a very short beak.

Habitat Restricted to the cold, shallow waters along the coast of Chile. Its range extends from Cape Horn, 55° South, to south of Valparaíso, 33° South. It seems to prefer more turbulent coastlines and fast-flowing estuaries and channels.

Behaviour A secretive, reclusive species, the Chilean dolphin is one of the smallest of all cetaceans and is not regularly observed. They swim with an undulating motion which is not unlike sea-lions and have been observed bow-riding passing ships in the north of its range. Not so in the south, where illegal hunting for crab bait has made it wary. Little information exists about this species and there have been no detailed studies.

Reproduction Unknown.

Diet Fish, squid and crustaceans.

Threats Hunted for crab bait.

Max length 1.7 m.

Max weight 65 kg.

Risso's Dolphin

Grampus griseus

Other Names Grey dolphin, Grampus.

Description A very large, robust dolphin with dark, scarred body and white belly. It has a distinctive rounded head and short beak which gives it an unmistakable profile. Other important features include a large sickle-shaped, upright, dorsal fin and dark pointed pectoral fins and flukes.

Habitat Found worldwide in deep tropical, sub-tropical and warm temperate waters. It has also been observed in enclosed seas such as the Mediterranean. Despite its widespread distribution, Risso's dolphin has not been studied in detail and little is known about the extent of its range or size of stocks.

Behaviour The unusual lateral scarring could be due to bite marks from other Risso's dolphins or (more likely) from scratches made by their main food source, the squid. They are often observed in smaller groups of up to 20 but also gather together into huge pods numbering thousands of individuals.

Reproduction Unknown.

Diet Mainly squid, some fish.

Threats Hunted in Asia and caught in fishing nets.

Max length 3.9 m.

Max weight 500 kg.

Rough-toothed Dolphin
Steno bredanensis

Other Names Slopehead.

Description An unusual looking species which is slightly reptilian in appearance. Its name derives from fine wrinkles on the enamel caps of its teeth. A slender dolphin, it has a broad, sloping forehead with no visible discontinuity around the beak and light-coloured patches which may be the result of attacks by squid or cookie-cutter sharks. Its cape is dark grey, with lighter grey flanks and a white belly. The tip of the beak is often white and dark patches surround the eyes.

Habitat A deep water species found in tropical, sub-tropical and warm temperate waters worldwide. It can only be observed inshore around sea mounts or oceanic islands and has not been studied in any detail. There is little information currently available about this species.

Behaviour Rough-toothed dolphins are usually observed swimming in small groups of 10-20 individuals and are often accompanied by other dolphins. They are not an acrobatic species but have been observed bow-riding.

Reproduction Unknown.

Diet Squid, octopus and fish.

Threats They are hunted in many parts of their range, especially in Asia and West Africa. Also entanglement in fishing nets.

Max length 2.7 m.

Max weight 160 kg.

48

Atlantic Hump-backed Dolphin

Sousa teuszii

Other Names Cameroon Dolphin.

Description A robust dolphin with an elongated hump on its back between body and dorsal fin. This species is large, robust, and has an ungainly, top-heavy appearance with a long narrow beak. It has mid-grey upper flanks which gradually lighten downwards to almost white around the belly.

Habitat An inshore species which spends most of its time in shallow water, typically less than 25 m deep. They are also commonly observed around river estuaries, deltas and mangrove swamps in slow-moving or static water. Their precise range is not clear, but there are confirmed groups in the tropical and sub-tropical coastal waters of West Africa. Presented here as a separate species, current research suggests that they may be the same species as the Indo-Pacific Hump-backed dolphin.

Behaviour They are often observed swimming with other dolphins, notably Bottlenose and Spinners. Despite their size and affinity with the gregarious Bottlenose, they tend to avoid boats and do not bow-ride.

Reproduction Calves every three years, gestation 10-12 months.

Diet Squid, octopus and fish.

Threats Entanglement in fishing nets and destruction of marine environment.

Max length 2.8 m.

Max weight 260 kg.

Indo-Pacific Hump-backed Dolphin

Sousa Chinensis

Other Names Chinese White dolphin or Pink Dolphin.

Description A robust dolphin with an elongated hump on its back between body and dorsal fin. It varies greatly in colour and appearance depending on location. Hump size can vary from pronounced to no hump at all and colour can be light grey, white or pink. Stocks around the South China Sea are notably white or bright pink, have little or no hump and a pronounced dorsal fin. By contrast, dolphins living around the Indonesian coastline have a pronounced fatty hump and very small dorsal fin.

Habitat An inshore species which spends most of its time in shallow water, typically less than 25 m deep. They are also commonly observed around river estuaries, deltas and mangrove swamps. Their extensive range reaches from Northern Australia to Southern China, Indonesia, Sumatra and around the Indian Ocean basin.

Behaviour They are often observed swimming with other species of dolphin; notably Bottlenose and sometimes Spinners. Shy and wary of humans they do not approach boats or bow-ride. Presented here as a separate species, current research suggests that they may be the same species as the Atlantic Hump-backed dolphin.

Reproduction Calves every three years, gestation 10-12 months.

Diet Squid, octopus and fish.

Threats Entanglement in fishing nets and destruction of marine environment.

Max length 2.8 m.

Max weight 260 kg.

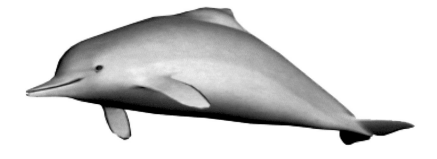

Tucuxi

Sotalia fluviatilis

Other Names Estuarine Dolphin.

Description A larger marine form of two sub-species (the other is found in rivers and lakes). It has a small, streamlined body, light grey cape, light grey flanks with distinctive white lobes and almost white or pinkish-white belly. Its beak is long and slender and it has a rounded trianglular dorsal fin. The Tucuxi (pronounced too-koo-shee) is sometimes mistaken for a small or young Bottlenose.

Habitat Commonly found in warm, shallow waters along the north eastern and eastern coasts of South America. They seem to prefer large estuaries and bays and are very common in the Amazon basin.

Behaviour Generally boisterous and energetic, the Tucuxi are very active at the surface and frequently breach, spyhop, splash and bow-ride. The riverine form has been extensively studied but little is known about the marine form.

Reproduction Unknown.

Diet Mainly fish.

Threats Entanglement in fishing nets, destruction of marine environment.

Max length 2.1 m.

Max weight 45 kg.

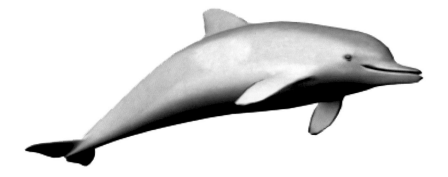

Irrawaddy Dolphin

Orcaella brevirostris

Other Names Snubfin Dolphin.

Description An unusual looking dolphin which resembles the Beluga whale and has a tiny, triangular dorsal fin, large rounded pectoral fins and a well rounded head with no beak. It has a darker grey cape with lighter flanks and underside.

Habitat Named after a river in Burma, the Irrawaddy dolphin prefers shallow river and coastal waters. It is particularly common in mangrove swamps and is widely distributed throughout the Indo-Pacific region from the Bay of Bengal to northern Australia. There are populations in the river Ganges in India, the Mekong in Vietnam and also in Cambodia, Laos and Borneo.

Behaviour Quiet and rather secretive, the Irrawaddy dolphin is difficult to observe and little is known about its behaviour. What is clear is the reduction in numbers due to coastal pollution and development projects.

Reproduction Unknown.

Diet Mainly fish but also squid, octopus, cuttlefish and crustaceans.

Threats Entanglement in fishing nets, destruction of marine environment.

Max length 2.8 m.

Max weight 130 kg.

26. Irrawaddy Dolphin

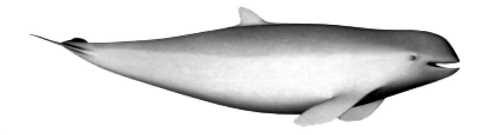

Northern Rightwhale Dolphin

Lissodelphis borealis

Other Names Pacific right-whale porpoise.

Description An unusual dolphin with a slender black body and no dorsal fin. It has a white belly which is generally not visible when below the surface and a white mark on the underside of its beak, which is short and slender. Rightwhale dolphins are the only species without a dorsal fin.

Habitat Found in cold temperate and sub-Arctic waters in the North Pacific between 30° North and 50° North. They prefer deep water and are rarely observed near land.

Behaviour Very streamlined body shape and low profile makes the Northern rightwhale dolphin fast and difficult to spot. They breach with low flat leaps which are generally only easy to see in calm, flat conditions. Often observed in the company of Pacific White-sided dolphins, they travel in large schools which can amount to thousands of individuals.

Reproduction Calves every two years. Gestation 12-13 months.

Diet Mainly fish and squid. Lanternfish is a particular favourite.

Threats Entanglement in fishing nets, some hunting with harpoons.

Max length 3.1 m.

Max weight 115 kg.

27. Northern Rightwhale Dolphin

Southern Rightwhale Dolphin

Lissodelphis peronii

Other Names Mealy-mouthed porpoise.

Description An unusual dolphin with no dorsal fin. It has a slender black upper body, white lower flanks and pectoral fins. Its black and white contoured pattern is clearly visible when below the surface and it has a short, stocky white beak. Rightwhale dolphins are the only species without a dorsal fin.

Habitat Found exclusively in cold temperate and sub-Antarctic waters across the entire southern hemisphere. They have been seen in subtropical latitudes following cold currents (such as the Humboldt) which flow up from the Antarctic. They are rarely observed near land.

Behaviour Very streamlined body shape and low profile makes the Southern rightwhale dolphin a fast swimmer and difficult to spot. They breach with low flat leaps which are generally only easy to see in calm, flat conditions. They travel in large schools of up to 1000 individuals and have been observed in the company of dusky dolphins and long-finned pilot whales.

Reproduction Unknown.

Diet Mainly fish, also squid.

Threats Entanglement in fishing nets, hunting for crab-bait in Chile.

Max length 3 m.

Max weight 120 kg.

Pygmy Killer Whale

Feresa attenuata

Other Names Slender blackfish, Slender pilot whale, Lesser killer whale.

Description The Pygmy Killer whale is known to be aggressive toward other cetaceans. It has a robust dark coloured body, with black cape, dark grey flanks, a light patch on its belly and light colouring on the lips and sometimes on the chin. It has a well-rounded head with no beak and a prominent, falcate dorsal fin.

Habitat Worldwide distribution in warm temperate, subtropical and tropical waters. They are a deep water species and are only observed close to the shore around mid-ocean islands.

Behaviour Aggressive cetacean which has been known to attack smaller dolphins and porpoise. Widely distributed but not closely studied, little is known about the habits of this species. It is often seen in groups of up to 50 individuals, travelling line-abreast. When approached they bunch together and quickly move away. Although there have been reports of bow-riding, the Pygmy Killer is neither social nor acrobatic and generally prefers to be left alone. It can be confused with the similar (slightly larger) Melon-headed whale but if there are a small number of individuals in the group then they are almost certain to be Pygmy Killers.

Reproduction Unknown.

Diet Mainly fish and squid.

Threats Entanglement in fishing nets.

Max length 2.6 m.

Max weight 170 kg.

False Killer Whale

Pseudorca crassidens

Other Names Pseudorca, False pilot whale.

Description A large, slender species which has been known to attack other cetaceans. Uniformally dark grey/black except for lighter patches on the throat and chest. It has a rounded head, no beak, and the male has a melon which overhangs its lower jaw.

Habitat Worldwide distribution in warm temperate, subtropical and tropical waters, including enclosed seas such as the Mediterranean. They prefer deep water and are only observed close to the shore around oceanic islands.

Behaviour An aggressive species which has been known to attack other dolphins and young whales. It is often seen in groups of up to 20 individuals and despite its aggressive temperament will happily swim with schools of Bottlenose dolphin. The False Killer is a fast and active swimmer and often breaches when coming to the surface. In addition to catching fish, it will readily steal from nets and for this reason has earned a bad reputation with fishermen. False Killers are susceptible to strandings and large groups numbering hundreds of individuals have been found on beaches.

Reproduction Calving interval seven years. Gestation 14-16 months.

Diet Mainly fish and squid. Known to attack other cetaceans.

Threats Entanglement in fishing nets.

Max length 6 m.

Max weight 2 tonnes.

30. False Killer Whale

Melon-headed Whale

Peponocephala electra

Other Names Many-toothed blackfish, Electra dolphin, Little Killer Whale.

Description The Melon-headed whale has a streamlined dark grey/black body with a black dorsal fin and cape. The head is narrow and pointed with no beak and light colouring around the lips. It generally has a white patch on its underside.

Habitat Worldwide distribution in sub-tropical and tropical waters. They are always seen in deep water and are only observed close to the shore around oceanic islands.

Behaviour Though widely distributed throughout the tropical seas, it tends to avoid contact with humans and sightings are not common. They tend to live in large groups numbering hundreds of individuals and have been seen swimming in mixed schools with Fraser's dolphins.

Reproduction Unknown.

Diet Mainly fish and squid.

Threats Entanglement in fishing nets.

Max length 2.7 m.

Max weight 210 kg.

31. Melon-headed Whale

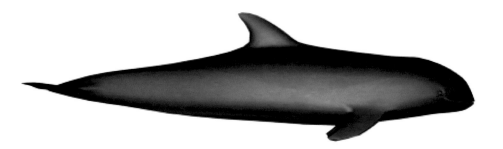

Long-finned Pilot Whale

Globicephala melas

Other Names Blackfish, Pothead whale.

Description It has a long, stocky dark grey/black body with a round head and prominent, bulbous melon. There is no beak and a light stripe sometimes runs from behind the eye to the front of the dorsal fin, which is short, stocky and is set forward on the body. As its name suggests, the long-finned Pilot whale has exceptionally long pectoral fins. Its underside is white. Males are considerably larger than females.

Habitat Two populations exist, one in the North Atlantic and western Mediterranean and the other in the Southern Ocean. They can both be found in cold, deep water.

Behaviour Long-finned Pilot whales live in small groups of around 10 to 20 individuals. They sometimes congregate into very large groups and strand more than any other cetacean. Mass strandings can involve hundreds of animals.

Reproduction Calves every 3-5 years. Gestation twelve months.

Diet Mainly fish and squid. Some crustaceans.

Threats Entanglement in fishing nets. The annual Faroe whale hunt accounts for around 1000 animals.

Max length 6.3 m (male)
4.8 m (female).

Max weight 3 tonnes.

Short-Finned Pilot Whale

Globicephala macrorhynchus

Other Names Blackfish, Pacific Pilot whale, Pothead whale.

Description Slightly larger then the long-finned, it has a robust dark grey/black body with a round head and prominent, bulbous melon. There is no visible beak. A light diagonal stripe runs from behind the eye and it has a pale saddle patch behind the dorsal fin, which is stocky, rounded and is set forward on the body. It has much shorter flippers than the long-finned pilot whale. Males are larger, have a more pronounced melon and a larger dorsal fin.

Habitat There is little or no geographical overlap with the long-finned species. Short-finned pilot whales prefer tropical, sub-tropical and warm temperate waters and are found worldwide. Absent from the Mediterranean, they are common around oceanic islands like the Azores and the Canaries.

Behaviour Short-finned pilot whales are social animals and live in groups that number 10-90 individuals. These groups often come together to form very large schools (sometimes hundreds of animals). The family groups have close bonds and they remain together for life. Individuals only leave to mate with other groups and hence prevent in-breeding.

Reproduction Calves every 5-8 years. Gestation 15-16 months.

Diet Mainly squid. Some fish and crustaceans.

Threats There are annual whale hunts in Japan and several hundred may be killed.

Max length 7.2 m (male)
5.1 m (female).

Max weight 4 tonnes.

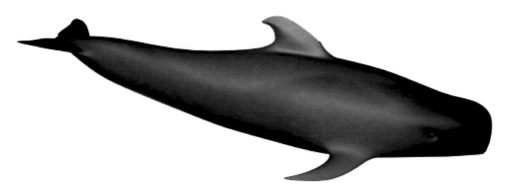

Orca

Orcinus orca

Other Names Killer Whale.

Description It has a very large, robust jet black body with brilliant white patches behind each eye. The underside is also white with rear-pointing lobes on each flank. Pectoral fins are large, flat and paddle-shaped and the dorsal fin is large, triangular and in the male is very tall (can reach 1.8 m). It has a grey or grey/blue saddle patch behind the dorsal fin. Despite its robust shape the Orca is very streamlined and is capable of swimming at high speed over long distances.

Habitat One of the most wide-ranging mammals on earth. Its population is distributed in all seas and oceans from the tropics to the Arctic and Antarctic.

Behaviour Extensively studied in a number of locations. They live in closely knit family groups (pods) which stay together for life. Behaviour and hunting techniques vary greatly and depend on the location and type of prey available. Pods may contain a number of different generations. They are intelligent, flexible, co-operative dolphins that make the best of their chosen environment. They are the largest member of the dolphin family and also the fastest swimmers, capable of achieving 50 km/h or more over significant distances.

Reproduction Calves every five years. Gestation 15-18 months.

Diet Extremely varied. Includes fish, squid, other cetaceans and marine mammals and even birds.

Threats Some are killed by fishermen.

Max length 9.0 m (male)
7.7 m (female).

Max weight 9 tonnes.

Vaquita

Phocoena sinus

Other Names Gulf of California porpoise.

Description A very small, shy dolphin which is perhaps the most endangered species of cetacean. It has a very small but stocky body, a shaded grey cape and lighter flanks. Its underside is white. The triangluar dorsal fin is slightly falcate. It has a rounded head, no beak and a dark line runs from its mouth to the the leading edge of its pectoral fins.

Habitat The most restricted distribution of any dolphin. It lives exclusively in the northern part of the Gulf of California (western Mexico). It is most often observed in the Colorado river delta and is only found in shallow water. A shy species, it does not seem to breach and avoids boats and human contact, hence few people have ever seen a live Vaquita. There may not be more than a thousand in existence and without more strenuous conservation efforts they are likely to become extinct.

Behaviour Due to its shy nature and very limited numbers, little is known about the behaviour of the Vaquita.

Reproduction Thought to calve every year. Gestation possibly 10-11 months.

Diet Fish, squid and crustaceans.

Threats Unknown.

Max length 1.5 m.

Max weight 55 kg.

35. Vaquita

Harbour Porpoise
Phocoena phocoena

Other Names Common porpoise, Puffer.

Description A small species which is fairly robust and has a shaded dark grey body with lighter underside. Its head is small with no beak and it has an upturned mouth with a dark stripe which connects with the pectoral fins. Its triangular dorsal fin is set towards the rear of the body.

Habitat Found in cool temperate and sub-Arctic waters in the northern hemisphere. A coastal species, it is rarely seen far from land and frequents shallow estuaries and bays.

Behaviour The Harbour porpoise is one of the commonest and most widely studied cetaceans. However, it rarely shows itself, is wary of boats and does not breach. It is often seen coming to the surface to breathe, the dorsal fin repeatedly rolling slowly out of the water and then disappearing again. The blow of the Harbour porpoise is rarely seen but it has a distinct sneeze-like sound that has given rise to the name 'Puffer' or 'Puffing Pig'. Like all porpoises, it has flat, spade-shaped teeth, quite unlike the conical teeth of dolphins. It has the shortest lifespan of all cetaceans and rarely lives beyond twelve years.

Reproduction Calves every 1-2 years. Gestation 10-11 months.

Diet Fish, squid, octopus and crustaceans.

Threats Principally, entanglement in gill nets but also some hunting.

Max length 1.9 m.

Max weight 80 kg.

36. Harbour Porpoise

Burmeister's Porpoise

Phocoena spinipinnis

Other Names Black porpoise.

Description A small, robust porpoise which has a shaded dark grey/black body and light underside. Its unique, backward leaning dorsal fin is set further back on the body than any other dolphin or porpoise. The head is small and flattened with no beak and it often has a dark stripe between the chin and pectoral fins.

Habitat A widely distributed South American species, its range stretches from Cape Horn to southern Peru on the western side and to southern Brazil on the eastern side. Not well studied, but current research suggests that it spends much of its time close to shore in the summer and offshore (out to 50 km) during the winter.

Behaviour They are rarely seen in groups and seem to spend much of their time swimming alone. Little is known about the habits of this small porpoise which is thought to be fairly widespread. Currently no conclusive data on population size exists.

Reproduction Probably calves every 1-2 years. Gestation 11-12 months.

Diet Fish, some squid and crustaceans.

Threats Widespread hunting. Entanglement in fishing nets.

Max length 1.9 m.

Max weight 105 kg.

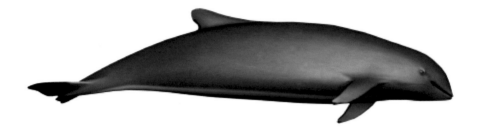

Spectacled Porpoise

Phocoena dioptrica

Other Names None.

Description The largest porpoise, it has a robust shape and a contoured jet black upper body, white flanks and white underside. It has a very distinctive, high, rounded dorsal fin (particularly in the male) and short, white pectoral fins. The head is small and rounded with no beak and it has black eyes surrounded by white 'spectacles'.

Habitat Found in the cold temperate and sub-Antarctic waters of South America, New Zealand and Australia. Its distribution is circumpolar and it has been observed in both coastal and offshore waters.

Behaviour Despite its distinctive markings, the Spectacled porpoise is rarely reported and little is known about its behaviour in the wild. Until 1976 only one confirmed live sighting had been made. Only a few at a time have ever been sighted, and occasional strandings indicate that it spends at least some of the year in shallower, coastal waters.

Reproduction Unknown.

Diet Fish, squid and crustaceans.

Threats Entanglement in fishing nets.

Max length 2.2 m.

Max weight 115 kg.

Finless Porpoise

Neophocaena phocaenoides

Other Names Black porpoise.

Description A small, slender porpoise which has a pale grey or grey/blue body and lighter underside. It has a dorsal ridge but no dorsal fin and comparatively large flippers. Like all porpoises, the head is small and rounded with no beak and it has a distinctive, rounded melon.

Habitat Finless porpoises are found in warm coastal waters and rivers around the Indo-Pacific rim. They are rarely seen far from land and seem to be at home at sea or in river systems.

Behaviour Instead of a dorsal fin, the Finless porpoise has a series of bumps (tubercles). Like other species of porpoise, the Finless rarely breaches and avoids boats and ships. Living close to shore and in rivers has affected the population size due to pollution, overfishing seabed deforestation and coastal disturbance.

Reproduction Calves every two years. Gestation about eleven months.

Diet Fish, squid, octopus, cuttlefish and crustaceans.

Threats Pollution, coastal exploitation and entanglement in fishing nets.

Max length 2.0 m.

Max weight 90 kg.

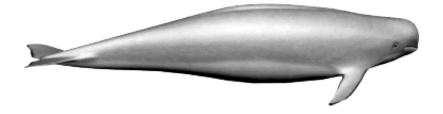

Dall's Porpoise

Phocoenoides dalli

Other Names Spray porpoise, Truei's porpoise.

Description A small but very stocky porpoise which has a distinctive shape and colour pattern. It has a black body and head with white patches on the flanks which extend to the underside. The dorsal fin is black with a prominent white tip. The pectoral fins and flukes are black. The head is very small compared with its body and it has an indistinct beak.

Habitat Found in the cool temperate waters of the North Pacific. It is a deep water species which spends much of its time out to sea. It only ventures close to shore in the winter and then only when the water is sufficiently deep.

Behaviour The fastest small cetacean, usually only breaking the surface momentarily and producing a 'rooster trail' of spray. It is extensively fished for meat by the Japanese, and upwards of 20,000 are killed each year. Unlike other porpoises, it will approach boats and ships and readily bow-rides. It does not breach but swims close to the surface at speeds of over 30 mph and provides hours of entertainment for whale watchers who go to see it.

Reproduction Calves every year. Gestation about 11-12 months.

Diet Fish and squid.

Threats Heavily hunted using drift nets.

Max length 2.4 m.

Max weight 200 kg.

Dolphin Animations *(for Windows Media Player)*

The last group of illustrations in the Dolphin Index are Windows movies that link different dolphin species to geographical locations and habitat.

41. Deep Water, North Atlantic Ocean

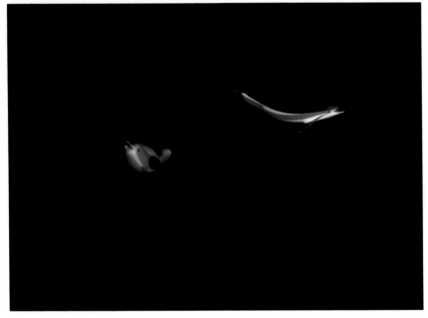

Species Included:

Atlantic White-Sided Dolphin
White-Beaked Dolphin

42. Deep Water, Tropical Seas

Species Included:

Spinner Dolphin
Clymene Dolphin
Short-Snouted Common Dolphin

43. Shallow Water, Tropical Seas

Species Included:

Common Bottlenose Dolphin
Atlantic Spotted Dolphin
Long-Snouted Common Dolphin

44. Deep Water, Sub-Tropical Seas

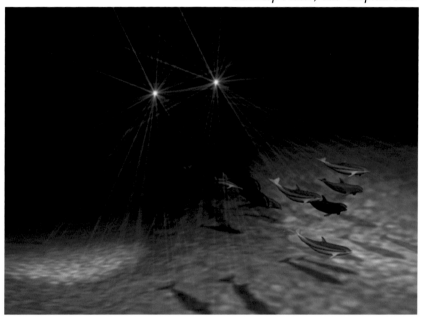

Species Included:

Fraser's Dolphin
Melon-Headed Whale

45. Deep Water, Antarctic Ice

Species Included:

Southern Rightwhale Dolphin
Hourglass Dolphin

Chapter 3

Conservation on the Web

Many species of oceanic dolphin are currently under threat and one or two are close to becoming extinct. The danger of extinction has been made worse by improvements in fishing technology. These allow fishermen to massively increase the size of catches and also the quantity and diversity of animals that are trapped. Many are drowned and discarded, killed as a by-product of an industry which may not only denude the seas of fish but many other species, including dolphins.

Hunting

In addition to the great whales, oceanic dolphins and porpoises are also hunted using a variety of harpoons, nets, explosives and rifles. The extent of world-wide hunting is impossible to ascertain but most references suggest that hundreds of thousands of animals are slaughtered every year.

Pollution

As world populations increase and coastal areas become more industrialised, so the problem of coastal and offshore pollution gets worse. In addition to the huge quantities of sewage and industrial waste that is pumped into the sea, there is also oil pollution due to shipping and offshore accidents. These can wreak havoc in vulnerable ecological areas such as arctic or antarctic regions and may affect many species of wildlife including cetaceans. As with hunting, the exact number of animals killed by pollutants each year is unknown, but it may contribute significantly to the decline of coastal species such as the Vaquita, Irrawaddy and Hump-backed dolphins.

Endangered Species

Oceanic dolphins are often very difficult to find and complex to study. With so little accurate data about dolphin numbers it is very difficult to say which are the most endangered species. However, the Vaquita is currently thought to be the most at risk species with a population of less than 1000. Hector's dolphin is the smallest cetacean and lives in the coastal waters of New Zealand. It is also seriously at risk and the total population may not be more than 3000.

Conservation and the Internet

Perhaps the best medium for finding and conveying information about whales and dolphins is the Internet. Many excellent cetacean web sites exist which contain up-to-date information about all aspects of whale and dolphin anatomy, behaviour, ecology etc. We have listed a few in a reference appendix, but these are no more than a start point and large quantities of information can be quickly collected by browsing the web.

Using this Book

We have deliberately designed this book to be used with a PC and to provide a platform for further study. It is a complete 3D reference for oceanic dolphins and includes basic facts about each species. Space has been left so that notes, scribbles and sketches can be added to the pages. In addition, the CD can be used to store data or image files which have been acquired from the web or other digital sources.

Web 3D Illustrations

Although protected by copyright, 3D animations from this book can be copied and included in non-commercial web sites. If you have access to a site which is involved in conservation or education, or you have a personal site and would like to include a conservation message, then you may find animated 3D illustrations very useful.

All of the data needed to create animated pages on the web are contained in the 'Dolphins in 3D/data' folder. If, for example, you require a copy of an interactive Common Bottlenose dolphin page on your site, open the data folder and upload commonbottlenose.html file and folders commonbottlenose and wf-player to your web server. Include a link from one of your own html pages to commonbottlenose.html file. If you would like to include a Common Bottlenose illustration in one of your existing web pages, copy the html code in the commonbottlenose html file between lines 'begin 3D presentation code' and 'end 3D presentation code'. Paste these lines into your page and upload it together with the commonbottlenose and wf-player folders.

Animation pages can also be included on your web site by uploading any of the html files animation1 to animation5 and setting up a link from an existing page to the uploaded animation page. To include animations in one of your web pages, copy the html code from an animation file between lines 'begin 3D presentation code' and 'end 3D presentation code'. Paste these lines into your html page and upload it.

The web is an ideal place to share ideas about dolphins and conservation of the marine environment. Text, pictures and animations can be brought together to provide compelling arguments that highlight the problems which influence the future of the dolphin and marine environment generally.

Appendices

Appendix A

Glossary

Beak - elongated mouth.
Belly - underside of dolphin.
Blow - exhaled cloud of water vapour.
Blowhole - nasal opening on top of head.
Blubber - layer of fat just beneath the skin.
Bow-riding - riding in the pressure wave of a ship or boat.
Breaching - leaping out of the water.
Cape - darker area over top surface of dolphin.
Cetacean - whale, dolphin or porpoise.
Crustacean - small marine invertebrate.
Dorsal fin - raised fin on back bone.
Drift net - fishing net that hangs in the water.
Falcate - degree of sweep of dorsal fin.
Flanks - side of dolphin.
Flipper - paddle shape limb on the front of dolphins (pectoral fin).
Fluke - flat horizontal tail of dolphin.
Gill net - small drift net.
Lobtailing - slapping flukes on the water.
Melon - a fatty organ bulging from the forehead of cetaceans.
Pectoral fin - see flipper.
Pod - family group of whales or dolphins.
Polar - region around north and south pole.
Porpoising - leaping out of the water while swimming at speed.
Purse-seine net - long net gathered around shoals of fish.
School - co-ordinated group of dophins.
Snout - see beak.
Spout - see blow.
Spyhop - dolphin raises its head out of the water to look around.
Tail stock - muscular region between dorsal fin and flukes.
Temperate - mid-latitude regions.
Tropical - lower latitude regions.
Wake-riding - swimming in the wake of a boat or ship.

Appendix B

References and Websites

MARK CARWARDINE	*Whales & Dolphins* ISBN 0-00-720547-3	2006
PETER GILL (EDITOR)	*Whales, Dolphins & Porpoises* ISBN 0-7054-3275-0	2000
MAURIZIO WURTZ & NADIA REPETTO	*Whales & Dolphins* ISBN 1-84037-043-2	1998

www.wdcs.org   *Whale & Dolphin Conservation Society*

www.mcsuk.org   *Marine Conservation Society*

www.csiwhalesalive.org   *Cetacean Society International*

www.dolphin-institute.com   *The Dolphin Institute*

Wild3D

3D Graphics & Publishing

www.wild3d.com